THE POWER OF STORY TELLING IN BUSINESS

BAMIDELE GODSPOWER TOMILOPE

DEDICATION

I dedicate this book to God Almighty for giving me the strength and will to write this book from the start to the end.

CONTENTS

CHAPTER ONE

The Power of Storytelling in Business

In the world of business, it's not just numbers and products that drive success; it's the stories we tell. Stories have been a fundamental part of human communication for millennia, and in the modern business landscape, they play an essential role in capturing the attention of customers, engaging employees, and differentiating your brand. This chapter will explore the profound impact of storytelling on businesses and set the stage for understanding how you can craft a compelling narrative to stand out and win in the competitive marketplace.

The Storytelling Advantage

Storytelling is not just a marketing buzzword; it's a powerful tool that taps into the very essence of human nature. From the earliest cave paintings to the modern-day corporate boardrooms, stories have been used to convey information, inspire action, and foster connections. They are memorable, relatable, and emotionally engaging, making them an ideal medium for businesses to communicate their purpose, values, and mission.

Why Stories Matter in Business

Connecting with Customers: Your customers aren't just buying a product or service; they're buying into a story. A well-crafted business narrative can create an emotional connection with your audience, leading to brand loyalty and advocacy.

Building Trust: Stories can humanize your brand. When you share stories about your journey, challenges, and successes, you build trust with your audience. People are more likely to trust businesses with a transparent and relatable narrative.

Effective Communication: Complex data and statistics can be overwhelming. Stories simplify and clarify your message, making it easier for customers and employees to understand and remember your core ideas.

The Psychology of Storytelling

To understand why stories are so effective in business, it's essential to delve into the psychology behind them. The human brain is wired to respond to narratives. When we hear a story, our brains release oxytocin, a hormone associated with bonding and trust. This chemical reaction makes us more receptive to the message and more likely to remember it.

Stories also engage multiple parts of the brain. They activate not only the areas responsible for language processing but also those linked to sensory experiences. This engagement creates a vivid and lasting impression.

In business, this psychological aspect is a powerful weapon. It allows you to influence customer behavior, inspire employees, and leave a lasting impact on your audience.

Setting the Stage for Crafting a Compelling Business Story

The power of storytelling in business is undeniable, but it's not enough to simply recognize its importance. In the chapters that follow, we will explore how to identify your unique business narrative, develop your storytelling skills, create an effective content strategy, and learn from successful case studies. By the end of this book, you will have the tools and knowledge needed to craft a compelling story that sets you apart and helps you win in the competitive world of business. Let's begin the journey of becoming a successful business storyteller.

Building Trust: Stories can humanize your brand. When you share stories about your journey, challenges, and successes, you build trust with your audience. People are more likely to trust businesses with a transparent and relatable narrative.

Effective Communication: Complex data and statistics can be overwhelming. Stories simplify and clarify your message, making it easier for customers and employees to understand and remember your core ideas.

The Psychology of Storytelling

To understand why stories are so effective in business, it's essential to delve into the psychology behind them. The human brain is wired to respond to narratives. When we hear a story, our brains release oxytocin, a hormone associated with bonding and trust. This chemical reaction makes us more receptive to the message and more likely to remember it.

Stories also engage multiple parts of the brain. They activate not only the areas responsible for language processing but also those linked to sensory experiences. This engagement creates a vivid and lasting impression.

In business, this psychological aspect is a powerful weapon. It allows you to influence customer behavior, inspire employees, and leave a lasting impact on your audience.

Setting the Stage for Crafting a Compelling Business Story

The power of storytelling in business is undeniable, but it's not enough to simply recognize its importance. In the chapters that follow, we will explore how to identify your unique business narrative, develop your storytelling skills, create an effective content strategy, and learn from successful case studies. By the end of this book, you will have the tools and knowledge needed to craft a compelling story that sets you apart and helps you win in the competitive world of business. Let's begin the journey of becoming a successful business storyteller.

CHAPTER TWO

Crafting Your Unique Business Narrative

Your business has a story waiting to be told. This chapter will guide you through the process of discovering and crafting your unique business narrative. Your story is more than just the products or services you offer; it's the essence of your brand, reflecting your values, mission, and the impact you aim to make. By the end of this chapter, you'll have a solid foundation to build your compelling business story.

The Essence of Your Business Story

Before you can craft your business story, you need to understand what lies at its core. Your business narrative should answer essential questions:

What is your mission? Why does your business exist beyond making a profit? What positive change do you seek to bring to the world?

What are your core values? What principles guide your business's decisions and actions?

What is your Unique Selling Proposition (USP)? What makes your business stand out in the market? What do you offer that others don't?

Who is your target audience? Whom do you want to connect with through your story? Understanding your audience is crucial for crafting a narrative that resonates with them.

Defining Your Mission and Values

Your mission is the driving force behind your business. It's the reason you get up every morning and work tirelessly. It goes beyond making money and focuses on the positive change you aim to create. Take the time to clarify your mission. Consider the impact you want to have on your customers, your community, or even the world.

Your core values are the guiding principles that shape your business's culture and behavior. These values should reflect what you stand for and what you won't compromise on. Some businesses value honesty, innovation, sustainability, or customer-centricity. Identify the values that resonate with your mission and set your business apart.

Unique Selling Proposition (USP)

In a crowded marketplace, you need to offer something distinctive to capture your audience's attention. Your USP is that unique quality or feature that sets you apart from competitors. It might be superior quality, exceptional customer service, innovative technology, or a commitment to sustainability. To craft a compelling narrative, you must identify and embrace your USP, making it a central element of your story.

Understanding Your Target Audience

Your story won't connect with everyone equally. Different audiences have diverse needs, preferences, and values. To craft a compelling business narrative, you must have a deep understanding of your target audience. Consider the following:

Demographics: Who are your ideal customers in terms of age, gender, location, income, and education?

Psychographics: What are their interests, values, beliefs, and lifestyle choices?

Pain Points: What problems or challenges does your audience face that your business can solve?

Aspirations: What are the hopes, dreams, and goals of your audience?

By identifying and empathizing with your target audience, you can tailor your narrative to resonate with them on a personal level.

Crafting Your Business Narrative

With a clear understanding of your mission, values, USP, and target audience, it's time to craft your business narrative. Your story should weave these elements into a compelling and coherent narrative that engages, informs, and inspires.

In the following chapters, we'll delve into storytelling techniques and practical exercises to help you build a narrative that brings your business to life. By the end of this journey, you'll have a well-defined and impactful business story that distinguishes you in the marketplace.

CHAPTER THREE

Storytelling Techniques and Tools

Now that you've clarified the essence of your business and have a solid foundation for your narrative, it's time to explore the techniques and tools that will bring your story to life. This chapter delves into the heart of storytelling, offering guidance on how to craft a compelling and memorable business narrative that captivates your audience and differentiates your brand.

Choosing the Right Storytelling Technique

Storytelling comes in various forms and styles, and choosing the right one for your business narrative is essential. Here are some popular storytelling techniques:

The Hero's Journey: This classic storytelling structure, popularized by Joseph Campbell, involves a hero (your business or customers) who embarks on a transformative journey, faces challenges, and emerges triumphant. It's a powerful way to inspire your audience.

The Problem-Solution Narrative: Identify a problem your audience faces, then present your business as the solution. This technique showcases how your products or services can make a positive impact in the lives of your customers.

Customer Success Stories: Share stories of satisfied customers who have experienced real benefits from your products or services. These testimonials serve as social proof and can be highly persuasive.

Behind-the-Scenes Stories: Take your audience on a journey behind the curtain to see how your business operates. This transparency can build trust and showcase your commitment to quality and integrity.

Origin Stories: Narrate the story of how your business came into existence. This personal touch humanizes your brand and can create a deeper connection with your audience.

The Power of Emotion in Storytelling

Emotions are a central element of any compelling story. They engage your audience on a personal level and make your narrative more relatable. Here's how to leverage emotions in your business story:

Identify the Emotion: Determine the key emotion you want to evoke in your audience. Is it joy, empathy, inspiration, or trust? Tailor your story to evoke this specific emotion.

Character Development: Create relatable characters within your story, whether they are customers who have overcome challenges or employees who are passionate about your mission. These characters can help evoke the desired emotion.

Conflict and Resolution: Every great story includes a conflict that is resolved. This journey from adversity to success is emotionally engaging. Highlight challenges your business has faced and how you've overcome them.

Visual and Auditory Elements: Use visuals, music, and other sensory elements to enhance the emotional impact of your story, especially in video or multimedia formats.

Practical Exercises to Develop Your Storytelling Skills

Crafting an engaging business narrative takes practice. Here are some exercises to help you hone your storytelling skills:

Story Mapping: Create a visual map of your story's structure, including the beginning, middle, and end. Ensure that your narrative flows logically and maintains the audience's interest.

Pitch Practice: Summarize your business story in a short elevator pitch. This exercise forces you to distill your narrative to its core, making it more impactful.

Tell Personal Anecdotes: Share personal stories within your business story. This adds authenticity and humanizes your brand.

Storytelling Workshops: Attend storytelling workshops or seek guidance from professionals to refine your skills further.

Remember, storytelling is an art that evolves over time. Keep refining and adapting your narrative as your business grows and changes. Your story should remain aligned with your mission, values, and the evolving needs of your audience.

In the following chapters, we'll explore how to integrate your narrative into a comprehensive content strategy, distribute it effectively, and measure its impact on your business success. Your journey to becoming a masterful business storyteller has just begun.

CHAPTER FOUR

Building an Effective Content Strategy

Crafting a compelling business narrative is just the beginning. To leverage the power of storytelling for success, you must integrate your narrative into a comprehensive content strategy. In this chapter, we'll explore how to design a content strategy that aligns with your business story, establish a content calendar, choose the right distribution channels, and measure the impact of your storytelling efforts.

Content Strategy and Your Business Narrative

Your content strategy should revolve around your business narrative. Every piece of content you create, whether it's a blog post, social media update, video, or email, should reinforce and extend your narrative. This consistent messaging builds brand recognition and trust.

Here's how to integrate your business narrative into your content strategy:

Core Messaging: Ensure that the core messaging of your content aligns with your mission, values, and USP. Your audience should immediately recognize your story in everything you share.

Narrative Elements: Infuse storytelling elements like characters, conflict, and resolution into your content. These elements engage your audience and make your messages more memorable.

Visual Consistency: Maintain a consistent visual style that reflects your brand's story. This includes colors, fonts, imagery, and design elements.

Tone and Voice: Your narrative sets the tone and voice for your content. Whether it's casual and friendly or formal and informative, ensure consistency in your messaging.

Establishing a Content Calendar

Consistency is key in content creation. A content calendar helps you plan and organize your content to ensure that it aligns with your narrative. Here's how to create an effective content calendar:

Frequency: Determine how often you'll publish content. This can be daily, weekly, or monthly, depending on your resources and audience expectations.

Content Types: Define the types of content you'll produce. This can include blog posts, videos, social media updates, podcasts, or newsletters.

Topics: Align your content topics with your business narrative. Plan a mix of content that educates, inspires, entertains, and engages your audience.

Timing: Consider the timing of your content. Some topics may be more relevant during specific seasons or events, so plan accordingly.

Distribution: Decide how and where you'll distribute your content. Your distribution channels should reflect the preferences of your target audience.

Leveraging Different Distribution Channels

Your narrative should be visible across various distribution channels to reach a broader audience. Here are some common distribution channels:

Website: Your business website is a central hub for your narrative. It should house your core story and offer easy access to other content.

Social Media: Utilize social media platforms that resonate with your audience. Share content that reinforces your narrative and engages your followers.

Email Marketing: Email newsletters are an effective way to deliver content directly to your audience, keeping them engaged and informed.

Video Platforms: Platforms like YouTube, Vimeo, or TikTok offer opportunities to share video content that brings your narrative to life.

Blogs and Publications: Guest posting on industry blogs or submitting articles to relevant publications can expand your reach and establish your expertise.

Measuring the Impact of Your Storytelling Efforts

To gauge the effectiveness of your business narrative and content strategy, you need to measure your efforts. Key performance indicators (KPIs) that can help you assess the impact of your storytelling include:

Engagement: Monitor the number of likes, comments, shares, and overall interaction with your content. High engagement indicates that your story resonates with your audience.

Website Traffic: Use tools like Google Analytics to track the traffic driven by your content. Analyze which pieces of content are most effective at bringing visitors to your site.

Conversion Rates: Measure how your content contributes to conversions, such as product purchases, sign-ups, or inquiries. Effective storytelling often leads to higher conversion rates.

Brand Recognition: Assess your brand's recognition and recall among your audience. Surveys and brand tracking can provide valuable insights.

Customer Feedback: Encourage feedback from your customers and audience to understand their perception of your narrative and its impact on their decision-making.

In the next chapter, we will explore successful case studies and real-world examples of businesses that have effectively leveraged storytelling for their success. By studying their journeys, you can gain inspiration and insights to further refine your own business narrative and content strategy. Your path to becoming a masterful business storyteller is well underway.

CHAPTER FIVE

Storytelling in Action: Case Studies and Success Stories

To truly appreciate the power of storytelling in business, let's dive into real-world case studies and success stories. In this chapter, we will explore the journeys of businesses that have effectively harnessed the art of storytelling to stand out, engage their audience, and win in the competitive marketplace. By studying their experiences, you can gain valuable insights and inspiration for crafting your compelling business narrative.

Case Study 1: Apple Inc. - The Story of Innovation

Apple Inc. is a prime example of a company that has masterfully integrated storytelling into its brand. Their narrative centers around innovation and challenging the status quo. From their famous "Think Different" campaign to the product launches led by Steve Jobs, Apple has consistently reinforced its story of being a game-changer in the tech industry. The emotional connection created through these narratives has led to intense brand loyalty and a dedicated customer base.

Key Takeaway: Apple's success demonstrates how a compelling narrative can shape a brand's identity and foster customer loyalty.

Case Study 2: Dove - Real Beauty Campaign

Dove's "Real Beauty" campaign challenged conventional beauty standards by promoting a more inclusive and authentic definition of beauty. Through videos, advertisements, and social media content, Dove conveyed a powerful narrative about self-acceptance and celebrating individuality. This narrative not only resonated with their audience but also drove a significant increase in sales.

Key Takeaway: Dove's campaign showcases the impact of aligning your narrative with a meaningful social cause and values shared by your audience.

Case Study 3: Patagonia - Environmental Stewardship

Patagonia, a company in the outdoor apparel industry, has woven a powerful narrative of environmental stewardship into its brand. Their commitment to sustainability and ethical practices isn't just a **marketing ploy;** it's a core part of their story. By sharing their journey, environmental initiatives, and challenges, Patagonia has attracted environmentally conscious consumers who align with their values.

Key Takeaway: Patagonia's success demonstrates that authenticity in storytelling, particularly when it involves social or environmental responsibility, can differentiate your brand and attract a dedicated customer base.

Case Study 4: Airbnb - Building Trust Through Personal Stories

Airbnb, a platform for home-sharing, recognized that trust is a significant factor for its users. They implemented a strategy where hosts and guests could share personal stories and experiences on their platform. This humanized the brand and built trust among users. Airbnb's narrative became one of connection and belonging, reinforced by personal accounts and testimonials.

Key Takeaway: Airbnb's success highlights how personal stories and user-generated content can enhance trust and build a community around your brand.

Case Study 5: Coca-Cola - Creating Emotional Connections

Coca-Cola's storytelling strategy revolves around creating emotional connections. Their iconic holiday ads, featuring polar bears and heartwarming stories, have become synonymous with the joy of the season. By tapping into universal emotions, Coca-Cola's narrative transcends cultural boundaries and has made them a global household name.

Key Takeaway: Coca-Cola demonstrates the power of evoking emotions through storytelling to establish a deep and enduring connection with customers.

Key Insights from Successful Business Storytelling

Authenticity matters: Authentic narratives, aligned with your brand's values, can build trust and long-term customer relationships.

Emotions drive engagement: Stories that tap into emotions have a more significant impact on your audience.

Consistency is key: Maintain a consistent narrative across all your content and communication channels to strengthen your brand's identity.

Focus on the audience: Understand your audience's needs and desires to create stories that resonate with them.

Use diverse storytelling techniques: Different stories can be used for different purposes, from inspiring your audience to demonstrating your problem-solving abilities.

By learning from these case studies and success stories, you can see how storytelling can be a potent tool for achieving business success. Crafting a narrative that aligns with your values, resonates with your audience, and differentiates your brand is a journey worth embarking upon. With the right narrative, you can stand out and win in the competitive world of business.

ABOUT THE AUTHOR

Bamidele Godspower Tomilope holds a degree of B.Sc Geography from Nasarawa State University, Keffi Nigeria. He is currently a Master's degree student of Geographic Information Science in the University of Ilorin, Kwara State Nigeria.